SHOP FRONTS

Alan Powers

SHOP FRONTS

Chatto & Windus
LONDON

Published in 1989 by
Chatto & Windus Ltd
30 Bedford Square
London WC1B 3SG

A CIP catalogue record for this book
is available from the British Library

ISBN 0 7011 3368 6

Photoset and printed in Great Britain by
Redwood Burn Limited, Trowbridge, Wiltshire

CONTENTS

PREFACE

Shop fronts can be the making or the undoing of historical streetscapes, yet their design history has been relatively little studied. Few shop fronts later than the early nineteenth century are listed, and from my experience as a caseworker for the Thirties Society, I have discovered how difficult it is to get mid twentieth-century shop fronts listed and preserved, although these are now some of the rarest. Belatedly, efforts are being made to consider the scale, colour and detailing of new shop fronts in towns like Bath, York and Harrogate. Architects are once more being called on to design classical wooden shop fronts, with some highly successful results, and I hope that the examples gathered here will inspire them.

Shop fronts fall victim to changes in commercial activity which cannot easily be prevented. A change of occupier, resulting in new paint colour and lettering, can bring an old shop front back to life, but more often something is lost. The famous shop of Fribourg and Treyer in Haymarket, although preserved as a physical object, no longer has the interest it possessed before this firm of tobacconists went out of business. Other historic shop fronts, like the equally famous 1750s one in Artillery Lane, Spitalfields, survive but are no longer in retail use.

This book considers the shop front as an aspect of architectural design rather than making a record of picturesque survivals. For this reason, I have only touched briefly on the economic and social history of shopping, and such associated aspects of shop front design as lettering, although in this respect, many modern shopfronts display their worst side. Many interesting old shops, from down-at-heel Georgian town centres to little village grocers, are disfigured by garish internally-lit plastic fascias.

I have concentrated on the single unit shop, since this has presented a consistent theme from the eighteenth century to the present. The design of department stores opens up another aspect of the subject too large to be treated here. I have tried to keep to retail shops, excluding public houses and purpose-built restaurants, banks and offices, although these all resemble shop fronts at certain times and were often designed and built in the same way.

In order to trace stages of stylistic evolution, it has been necessary to use a number of old photographs of shop fronts long vanished. Old photographs of surviving shop fronts are often preferable because today the view is spoilt by traffic bollards, signs and other impedimenta. The examples are predominantly in London, not only because it is where I live, but because the centre of London is unexpectedly rich in historic shop fronts.

I would like to thank Bridget Williams, Archivist for Sainsburys, Mr T. W. Baker-Jones, archivist for W. H. Smith, Mr P. I. Pegram of Pegram and Co., shopfitters of Camden Town, Frank Collieson of Heffers Bookshop, Cambridge, Colin Sorenson and Wendy Evans of the Museum of London, the staff of the Greater London Record Office and History Library, Dr Michael Stratton of the Institute of Industrial Archaeology, Ironbridge, the Beamish Museum, the National Monuments Record and the British Architectural Library for their assistance.

SHOP FRONTS

Origins

A shop front consists of a door and a window, and the earliest examples were little more than that, the window having shutters which formed a counter and a canopy, so that the wares could be laid out in the light, and transactions made through the window.

In the nineteenth century, when interest in the history of shop fronts first began, there were a number of contenders for the oldest shop front, all of them probably dating from the seventeenth century, such as the Old Bulk Shop at Temple Bar in London, demolished in 1846 (p. 35) – the 'bulk' referring to the projecting framework. Another was at No. 44 Fenchurch Street, and yet another in Macclesfield Street, Soho, thought to date from 1690. All have now disappeared. They were of antiquarian rather than architectural interest, and indicate how before the eighteenth century shop buildings were only occasionally considered an important part of the tradesman's investment. A great deal of trade was carried on in markets and fairs, there being long traditions associated with the buying of certain goods at different times of year. Shops served more often as artisan workshops. As Dorothy Davis writes, 'All the evidence on seventeenth-century London retailers points to a general acceptance of very slow turnover, very high profit margins, and, with a few notable exceptions, to a poor and precarious livelihood.'[1]

Yet by 1663, a visiting Frenchman could write that 'There is no city in the world that has so many and such fine shops. For they are large and their decorations are as valuable as those of the stage.'[2] This must refer principally to Cheapside, with its goldsmiths' shops

in almost uninterrupted succession along the south side, the most
magnificent shopping street of seventeenth-century London. The
shopkeepers' wives were also famous for sitting, splendidly dressed,
in the shop doorways, bantering with passers-by and attracting
custom. By the end of the century, this trade was beginning to move
to Holborn, to be replaced by milliners, booksellers and linen-
drapers.

One of the first 'shopping developments' was the upper gallery of
Sir Thomas Gresham's original Royal Exchange of 1568, originally
intended for merchants, but appropriated by traders in laces and fine
cloths when the merchants showed their preference for remaining
on ground level. Architecturally speaking, the actual shops were
very modest timber constructions. The success of the 'Pawne' at the
Royal Exchange led to its imitation in the Earl of Salisbury's New
Exchange in the Strand of 1608, intended solely for shops, which
enjoyed the height of its popularity in the Restoration.

Developments of this kind, and the unique phenomenon of the
'Rows' in Chester, originating in the thirteenth century for domestic
as well as commercial use, are subsidiary to the tradition of the shop
built into a normal house at ground level, and usually limited in
breadth by the party walls of the houses. The span of the shop front
was easily within the bearing capacity of a solid timber bressumer,
holding up the brickwork of the house front, and concealed behind
the fascia.

By 1700, the more luxurious shops in London had small-paned
windows of glass, set in a containing framework, but do not seem to
have been considered places to display the skills of the carpenter or
carver, although Defoe noted in 1732 the interiors with their
'painting and gilding, fine shelves, shutters, boxes, glass doors,
sashes and the like'.[3] Attention was instead concentrated on the
hanging signs, which were a special feature of London streets,
enormous in size, and hanging closely together, until their sudden
abolition as a public nuisance in 1762. This was not the end of

hanging signs, but thereafter they were controlled in size, and have survived more strongly as a tradition in Scotland.

Classical Design and the Consumer Revolution

It is from the Rococo period in the mid-eighteenth century that shop fronts begin to survive in sufficient numbers to make their history more definite. Their greater elaboration coincided with a definite acceleration in commercial activity and trade, particularly connected with an increase in what we now call consumer goods – articles of luxury and fashion rather than of necessity. As Neil McKendrick has written, 'The beauty of smallness had not been recognised as such in the eighteenth century, but the profitability of such unconsidered trifles as pins and nails, buttons and forks, knobs and knockers, pots and pans, hats and coats, gloves and shoes certainly had.'[4] The appearance and up-to-dateness of the shops in which such things were bought became increasingly important through the second half of the eighteenth century and beyond.

Bow windows were a favourite device in the second half of the eighteenth century for making the display more conspicuous, and for getting more light into the shop. No. 34 Haymarket, occupied from 1754 until recently by the tobacconists Fribourg and Treyer (p. 36), is a humbler example of the double bow front. Bow-fronted shops have long been appreciated as charming examples of the carpenter's design work, but seldom have architectural pretensions.

Protruding bows were contrary to strict classical taste, but they were in any case restricted under the London Building Act of 1774 to prevent fire and encroachment on the pavement. A projection of only ten inches or less was henceforth permitted for new buildings, although outside London regulation was more lenient.

The restriction of the bow must have created a greater problem in terminating the cornice. According to the rules, the mouldings cannot just be cut off, but have to have an architectural finishing. If the cornice is 'returned' at right angles with a mitred joint, the

conventional solution, the shop front below may lose one foot in
width at each end, a serious matter when the whole width may be
no more than fourteen feet. The solution may be simply to reduce
the projection of the cornice. The fine chemist's shop formerly
existing at No. 11 Norton Folgate in Spitalfields (p. 37) must have
been built before 1774, but already the cornice is delicate and slim.
The shop front is a bold piece of carpenter's design, with three
bows, the centre one being an unsupported projection over the
door. The basement must have been comparatively well-lit from the
balustraded stallboard, but the most striking feature is the spread
eagle over the door, a latter-day substitute for the lost hanging signs.
The miniaturised cornice and pilasters show how useful the Adam
neo-classical style was in succession to the mid-century Palladian
rococo, because of the liberties it permitted with the proportions of
the orders. As Sir John Summerson has noted, 'the Building Act
came at a time when ornamentation could perfectly well cope with
these restrictions.'5 William Pain's pattern books provide special
elongated versions of the orders for use on shop fronts, either as
pilasters or columns in the round, in conjunction with plates of
flattened bows much like those at No. 4 St Mary's Street, Stamford
(p. 38).

A common device for dealing with the cornice return was to
curve the ends of the frieze up towards the centre, with the profile
of a scotia moulding, producing a typical late-Georgian type of shop
front. This treatment occurs in the shop front formerly at No. 15
Cornhill, long famous as the confectioners Birch and Birch (p. 39),
before its removal to the Museum of London. The chief delight of
this front is the fine Adamesque decoration of beads and husks. A
later example of the swept ends, combined with paired bays
supported on thin consoles, is the shop front of c. 1820 from Creek
Street, Greenwich, also in the Museum of London (p. 40).

Classical architecture is in many ways ideally adapted to shop
front design, not least because the entablature provides a place to
write the name of the shop, and the cornice gives weather protection

to the windows. Outstanding among the more architectural shop
fronts of this period is No. 56 Artillery Lane, Spitalfields (p. 41),
probably built between 1756 and 1757. The interiors of this and the
neighbouring house are unusually magnificent, and the shop front
combines five columns of the Doric order with a pair of bow-
fronted windows, and a rococo cartouche over the shop door. As a
piece of classical architecture, it is hardly within the rules of design,
for the columns are not regularly spaced and the Doric entablature
should not curve out and in. The columns each support an airily
carved bracket, rather than appearing to bear the load of the
superstructure. Yet shop fronts, for most of their history, have
seldom conformed to the classical rules for the correct use of
columns, entablatures and mouldings, or even basic symmetry. One
reason for this is the variety of specific functions that have to be
incorporated, such as having two doors, one for the shop and one
for the private house, and the need to provide light for the basement
through grilles in the stallboard (the solid section of the shop front
beneath the windows).

The Artillery Row shop front illustrates some of the difficulties
involved in shop front design according to classical principles. The
private door has to go at one end of the shop front, corresponding
to the position it would occupy in a normal terrace house; behind it
is a hallway which leads to a staircase giving access to the house
above. The remaining architectural composition is then inevitably
off-centre in relation to the upper part of the house, unless the shop
door balances the house door. This is not commercially desirable,
however, as the customer wants to be sure of entering by the right
door. These enforced irregularities could be overcome by a variety
of ingenious methods, but for the most part, they do not seem to
have worried the carpenter-architects working from pattern books,
although the engraved designs usually suppressed the practical
problems.

The shop front of No. 1 Terrace Walk, Bath (p. 43), manages to
be much more regular. Because it is on a corner, the house can be

entered from the side street, and the shop front, with its Ionic
columns and triple arches with decorated spandrels, looks like a
plate from a pattern book by Gibbs. In the early twentieth century
it was 'restored' and the door put in the middle, while an earlier
photograph shows it on the right, with plate glass in the windows.

Shutters and Blinds

Another practical aspect of shop front design liable to be forgotten
is the use of shutters. Until the introduction of iron roller shutters
in the 1840s, these were a universal if troublesome feature of the
shopkeeper's life, persisting even to the present in old-fashioned
businesses like the Bond Street jewellers Tessiers or the wine-
merchants Berry Bros. in St James's Street (p. 42).

The shutters were normally carried in and out by the apprentices
at the beginning and end of each day, each being a tall wooden
framework with panels. They slotted into a groove under the
architrave and with pins into the ledge at the top of the stallboard.
The metal plates with holes for the pins can often be found under
the paint of old shop fronts. The whole set of shutters would
probably then be held in place by an iron strap, the fixings for
which can also often be found. In unusual cases, the design of the
window allowed space for the shutters to be kept outside during the
day.

Shutters were cumbersome, and the introduction of the roller
shutter in the 1830s was welcomed. These were made of iron ribs,
and could be pulled up or down by one man. They were first
installed by the Duke of Wellington at Apsley House, then in 1837
at Swan and Edgar, afterwards rapidly spreading in popularity. The
extra space needed behind the fascia for the roller shutter led to
fascias being built tilted forward. Roller blinds on springs, probably
introduced in the early nineteenth century, could also be fitted to
the cornice, with metal stays fixed to the pilasters on either side,
operated by a long boat-hook. George Scharf shows one on

Pocknall's Oyster Bar on the north side of the Strand in 1829, where it was obviously desirable to keep the goods cool. Blinds were useful for shading the customer and reducing reflections and glare in the window. There were complaints in the 1840s that they were hung with side aprons as low as five feet off the ground, making progress along the pavement extremely difficult.

Design and Display

Within the limits of the fourteen- to twenty-foot frontage, with a house above, the physical conditions governing shop front design from c.1750 to c.1840 remained remarkably constant, so that it is hard to date examples precisely. What is remarkable is the number of shop fronts from this period that have survived in good condition, compared to the poor survival rate for later periods. They have mainly survived in areas which went out of fashion in the later nineteenth century, so that shopkeepers did not have profits to lavish on alterations. Equally remarkable is the ingenuity with which the basic language of classicism was varied and improvised upon by unknown designers, corresponding to the varieties of design in china, textiles and metalwork of the same period.

The style of shop fronts was usually passed down the social and architectural hierarchy. In 1754 *The World* deprecated the spread of the chinoiserie-rococo style, with the result that there was 'from Hyde Park to Shoreditch scarce a chandler's shop or an oyster stall but has embellishments of this kind.' Unfortunately, few such examples have survived, although shop fronts continued to be capricious. The 1780s trade card of John Flude, Pawnbroker and Silversmith, of No. 3 Gracechurch Street (p. 45), shows a shop front ungoverned by architectural logic, but designed, as jewellers have continued to be, to show a profusion of objects in separate windows. A display case projects on brackets in front of the stallboard, making a three-sided showcase, with further display on the far side of the shop door. The cornice has 'Gothick' ornaments

and early neo-classical cartouches. 'The 'Gothick' pendant design
can be found on several charming shops still existing, one in
Woodbridge, Suffolk, at the top of Church Street, another in
Hungerford High Street, Berkshire, following the curve of two
remarkable 'free-form' bow windows.

In 1777, George Dance the Younger designed some shop fronts
for Finsbury Square, demonstrating the architect's restraining hand.
The elements were much the same as those used in doorcases –
carved brackets, cornices and fanlight glazing, the latter of
considerable delicacy, as demonstrated in numerous shop fronts in
York. The friezes of the bows there are often decorated with
festoons and drops in 'compo', a moulding material like putty.
There seems to have been little distinction between the quality of
workmanship applied to large and small shops. As already indicated,
the taste for highly priced luxury items helped the expansion of
shopping, and these were not necessarily large in themselves.

Some of the best depictions of shop fronts of this period are
found in the drawings of George Scharf, whose work has already
been mentioned, showing the great diversity of bows, curves and
serpentine fronts in streets like the Strand. A more schematic
representation is found in the series of street views drawn and
published by John Tallis between 1838 and 1840. The appearance of
the shop front was enhanced, by the time of the Regency, by
imitation marble and graining. As James Peller Malcolm wrote in
1810,

> The shopkeeper prides himself on the neatness of his shop front,
> his little portico, and the pilasters and cornices are imitations of
> Lydian, Serpentine, Porphyry and Verde Antico antique marbles.
> Those who have the good fortune to serve any branch of the
> Royal Family immediately place large sculptures of their several
> arms and supporters over their doors, and their own names and
> business in golden characters.[6]

The effect of royal patronage can be seen in the shop front of Mr

Burgess, Italian warehouseman, at No. 107 Strand, photographed in the 1890s (p. 46), with a splendid royal arms and an old-fashioned crowded window-display, while no fewer than six royal crests once decorated the doorway of Twinings' tea warehouse in the Strand (p. 47), not strictly a shop front, but a delightful survival, with its seated Chinamen supporting a British lion. Another remarkable sculptural ornament survives in York at the corner of Stonegate and Minster Gates, advertising a stationer and bookseller with Minerva supported on a pile of books. The design of this extensive shop front is a version of a popular device of having arch-headed windows with fanlight-style glazing. The pilasters have slender paired brackets with a leaf ornament, topped off by lion's head paterae, supporting the narrow cornice. No. 48 Stonegate, York (Taylor's Tea Rooms) is a simpler front in the same style, with a fine decorated fanlight.

Designs of this type form the greater part of *Designs for Shop Fronts*, published in 1792 by I. and J. Taylor, the spandrels of one of their designs being decorated with imitation curtains. One Gothic design is included, but apart from the use of interlaced Gothic glazing bars, as seen at No. 30 Trinity Street, Cambridge (p. 48), this style does not seem to have had the same popularity in commerce that it had in churches and houses.

A coat of arms provides a useful focus to the architectural composition, as in the double-fronted shop at No. 37 Stonegate, York (p. 49), with its unusually elaborate cornices over the bows, and a rather humble door in the centre.

There seems to have been little architectural differentiation between trades at this time. Instead, the shop window was packed with merchandise which helped the pedestrian to recognise what was on sale. As James Peller Malcolm wrote in 1810,

> The Goldsmiths and Jewellers and some Pawnbrokers indulge the public with view of diamonds, pearls, rubies, emeralds, gold and silver, in most fascinating quantities; but the watch-makers and

Glassmen eclipse all competition in the display of fanciful clocks, set in alabaster, *ormolu*, gold and silver, and the richest cut glass lighted by patent lamps at night. The Bookseller exposes copies of the most expensive works in his windows, and the Printsellers those of the best artists. The Undertaker covers his panes with escutcheons, crowns, coronets and mitres of gold ... The retailer of Quack Medicines covers every page of his shop windows with the bills of different compounders of nostrums, and the angles between the paper and the sashes with vivid transparent colours; and the Proprietors of Newspapers seize upon every battle or capture as fair opportunities for pasting large pieces of paper together which they inscribe 'Sixth edition' etc. and suspend from the top to the bottom of their casements.[7]

The packing of the window with goods has continued in old-fashioned shops up to the present. It was originally necessary because of the impossibility of lighting the interior as part of the display.

A London magazine reported a Frenchman's observation of 'this tone of quackery which shocks foreigners', but the reports of most foreign visitors were complimentary about the London shops, the *Souvenirs de Londres* remarking in 1824 that the variety and richness of the shops and their window displays distracted from the depressing uniformity of the soot-covered house fronts. The most impressive shops were in Oxford Street, the centre of fashion before Regent Street became its rival when constructed in the 1820s. In 1786, the traveller and diarist Sophie von La Roche described the scene:

Behind great glass windows absolutely everything one can think of is neatly, attractively displayed, in such abundance of choice as almost to make one greedy ... There is a cunning device for showing women's materials. Whether they are silks, chintzes or muslins, they hang down in folds behind the fine, high windows so that the effect of this or that material, as it would be in the ordinary folds of a woman's dress, can be studied.[8]

Gas lighting was introduced in 1792, replacing oil lamps and giving, by the standards of the time, a brilliant illumination to the street. Lighting was particularly necessary as shops usually stayed open until nine or ten o'clock at night. Until the improvements in street lighting in the 1920s and 1930s, coinciding with greater regulation in opening hours, shops continued to make their own blaze of light with great lamps on hanging brackets.

London and other fashionable towns were far in advance of the Continent. Neil McKendrick has written that

> the break with the past was very apparent. These new shops were in size, in appearance, and in scale of operations, the true precursors of their commercial descendants which serve our present society of mass consumption. These were not the mere hutches or mere stalls which so many contemporaries described as shops in the seventeenth century.[9]

So evidently splendid were they that one of Pitt's taxes in the French wars was levied on shops.

Parades and Arcades

The rise in the social status of shops was accompanied by attempts to include them as part of regular architectural compositions in new developments. Woburn Walk, near Euston Station, was built by the Bedford Estate in 1822, and is exceptional in its combination of elegant flat bow fronts, supported on brackets, with neo-classical house fronts above (p. 50). A development of this kind was too far away from the centre of fashion to be really successful, but fortunately it has survived.

At Cheadle, in Staffordshire, there is a remarkable terrace, built in 1819, at the top of the sloping market place, with five identical

single-bow shop fronts, each with an entrance door at the apex of
the bow – a style long since abandoned in London (p. 51). Examples
of such regular planning became more numerous in the early
nineteenth century, although they are now sometimes difficult to
detect because of later alterations. Indeed, it can be assumed that
any builder-developer would have aimed at the convenience of
uniformity, even if the commercial tenants later introduced their
own variations.

In the years after Waterloo, the Royal Opera Arcade (p. 52),
running from Pall Mall to Charles Street, was built as the first of a
new type of covered shopping development popularised in Paris
with the Palais Royal, where shops and cafés ran along the three
ranges of building enclosing the gardens. These were finished in
1786 to the designs of Victor Louis, and were an immediate success,
not least because of their blatant use by prostitutes.

In spite of the Haymarket's dubious reputation in the nineteenth
century, this aspect was not imitated in the Royal Opera Arcade,
one side of which served as cloakrooms for the theatre, the other
side for small luxury shops, with single bow fronts, designed by
John Nash. In 1865 Henry Mayhew described it as 'the arcade of
the melancholy-mad bootmakers'.[10]

Designed by Samuel Ware for Lord George Cavendish and
opened in 1819, the Burlington Arcade (p. 53), leading from
Piccadilly to Burlington Gardens was, and has remained, more
commercially active. It combines double and single shops with bow
fronts, and answering oriel windows in the upper storey. According
to Mayhew 'a friendly bonnet shop' offered other services in one of
these upper rooms, but the main trade, then as now, was in 'a
sublimate of superfluities ... and falbalas of all descriptions.'

In the words of J. F. Geist, the meticulous historian of the arcades
of the world, the Burlington Arcade was 'the first important arcade
in England with wide-reaching influence on the development of the
building type both in England and America'.[11]

An impressive collection of arcades, dating from the last quarter of the nineteenth century, exists in Leeds, but hardly any interesting shop fronts remain. Better examples are found in Newcastle in the Grainger Market, including the fascia of an original Marks and Spencer's Penny Bazaar. In London, the delightful Piccadilly Arcade of 1909 has distinctive windows of curved glass, rising from the ground through two storeys without a break, creating an effect like an undulating Regency seaside terrace.

Regency Classicism

In the design of individual shops, the effect of the Greek Revival from c.1810 onwards was to encourage a return to the use of the classical orders. Doric, Ionic, Corinthian and Composite are all found adding dignity and occasionally a rather absurd grandeur to shop fronts. No. 37 Soho Square (p. 54), although no longer a shop, has a fine Doric front presumably installed for Dulau, the foreign booksellers who came here in 1800. A slenderer version of Doric is found at No. 51 Lamb's Conduit Street, with an altered centre section resulting, presumably, in the loss of a column. It may originally have looked like the elegant, long-vanished shop front at No. 209 High Holborn (p. 55), with its handsome pair of double doors suggesting that this was not primarily designed for retail use. The entablatures of both of these have a 'swept' profile, with a simple architrave ornament. This is certainly more sensible than the proper Doric frieze with its triglyphs which prevent the use of lettering.

A fine Ionic shop front of c.1828 is No. 8 Argyle Street, Bath (p. 56), exceptional in projecting some four feet from the house front, over the basement area, allowing the columns to dominate the window. Another Greek Revival example from as late as 1849 is the pair of shops, Nos. 13 and 14 St Mary's Street, Stamford (p. 57), with a richly decorated anthemion frieze, carried round the curved corners, an effect not known in ancient Greece, but rich and beguiling in its setting. These shops form part of a deliberately

contrived street picture, comparable to a Corinthian pair in Craven
Road, Paddington.

One of the finest Corinthian shop fronts is Frank Cooper's in the
High Street, Oxford (p. 58), the home of the famous marmalade,
established here in 1840. It is an unusually tall shop front, allowing
proper scope to the proportions of the orders. Inside, it has fine
marbled Ionic columns. Corinthian and Composite, the showiest
orders of classical architecture, were inevitably popular with
tradesmen, appearing consistently up to about 1850. A fine example
is No. 43 Eastcheap (p. 58), notable for its antique-style double
doors on either side of the central window. In Richmond Avenue,
Barnsbury (p. 54), an 1830s shop front bizarrely combined
Corinthian columns with ogee glazing and other Gothic ornaments.

The desire to bring shop fronts within the province of the
architect can be seen in the work of J. B. Papworth (1775–1847), the
architect of Regency Cheltenham. He designed villas for successful
businessmen, and also their shops.

In 1822, Papworth designed the 'Brighton Pavilion' of shop
fronts, for F. and R. Sparrow, Tea Merchants, at No. 8 Ludgate Hill
(p. 60), although the chinoiserie is confined to the ornamentation of
the upper storeys of the house, in a manner irreverently recalling Sir
John Soane's refronting of No.13 Lincoln's Inn Fields. It was
uncommon to use the house front so boldly, although lettering and
devices like giant spectacles were applied from time to time, and
George Scharf recorded the remarkable Lardner's Blacking Factory
at No. 224 Strand, with ornamental boots, slippers and blacking
bottles. Papworth's design is like one of the stage shop fronts which
invariably figured in the harlequinades of Victorian pantomime,
with flaps ready to fly up at the touch of Harlequin's baton,
revealing some humorous topical 'gag' beneath.

Papworth's other shop fronts were more conventional, and in the
collection of his drawings, he can be seen trying to regularise the
empirical arrangements of a typical carpenter's design, particularly
in order to get the shop front centred on the house above. On

paper, the results are highly elegant, although they may have been difficult to use. Papworth sensibly abandoned the classical orders, and used the more adaptable vocabulary of pilasters, with Greek or Italianate detail (p. 62).

For Joseph Butterworth, the legal booksellers, Papworth made several designs for a shop-front at No. 43 Fleet Street (p. 62) between 1827 and 1828, trying a central door or two doors · separated by a central window. The ornamental detail is sparse but telling. The cross-section shows how the fascia is built forward from the bressumer that holds up the house front, and how a special display cabinet with a raked base for the books was built in.

At No. 115 Piccadilly (p. 62), Papworth designed an almost domestic front for Robert Hughes, an upholsterer and cabinetmaker, with paired doors flanking a central tripartite window and a verandah carried on four square piers. A particularly complete set of drawings from 1829–30 for Thompson and Fearon, Wine Merchants of No. 94 Holborn Hill (p. 64), has survived, showing details like the console bracket, of which four were ranged along the fascia supporting a cornice. These, with their idiosyncratic Greek Revival detailing, were among the predecessors of thousands installed by the end of the nineteenth century, nearly always just as end-stops without Papworth's careful thought about the appearance of carrying a load.

Papworth also experimented with iron construction, which made higher and airier shop fronts possible. The façades in Nash's Regent Street of the 1820s were designed on the thinnest iron supports in the expectation that the shop fronts would be frequently changed 'to please the demon of fashion', as James Elmes complained in the *Metropolitan Improvements* of 1827. New possibilities arose for the treatment of corners, as George Scharf shows in his drawing of a corner shop under construction in Hungerford Street in 1834. Brick arches are carried on thin iron stanchions, allowing for a well-lit mezzanine. Similar conversion works applied to existing shops in the suburbs frequently led to collapse in the 1830s and 1840s.

In 1834 J. C. Loudon's *Architectural Magazine* carried a short
and critical note on shop front design; although it commended the
use of consoles blocking off the ends of the cornice as 'very
consistent and handsome', this was evidently rare at that date.
George Scharf shows workmen moulding consoles on site for
application to a pub in 1843. It was clearly much cheaper to do this
than to have them carved in wood, which might in any case have
been in breach of the new Building Act after 1845. There is a
seemingly endless variety in the design of these consoles, some of
them being emblematic of the trade originally carried on, some
having human or lion heads. A fine example being the shop on the
corner in St Giles's Street, Oxford (p. 65).

A drawing from 1843 in the RIBA Collection by Harvey Lonsdale
Elmes, the designer of St George's Hall, Liverpool, shows a slightly
later stage in the evolution of the architect designed shop front. A
group of three houses in Lime Street, Liverpool (p. 62), is presented
with three alternative shop front designs, in the form of Venetian
windows, with doors to the sides. The arcaded treatment of the
building gives a greater impression of solidity, and overcomes the
habitual objection that shop fronts made the upper part of the
building appear to be supported almost entirely on glass.

Styles for Sale

Professional architects retained a considerable involvement with the
design of shop fronts through the first half of the nineteenth
century, but they were mostly from the more obscure levels of the
profession, such as George Maddox (1760–1843), who reputedly
designed the Grand Theatre, Moscow, but for a time left his mark in
London in shop fronts such as a chemist's at No. 165 Strand (now
demolished), whose four-pilastered front is just legible in the street
view by Tallis. Architects were certainly responsible for expanding
the existing range of styles and adding richer ornamentation. Pattern
books published by John Young and Thomas Faulkner in 1828 and

1831 respectively introduce more florid variations on Papworth's ornament, in the style sometimes known at the time as 'the fancy style'. In the words of H. S. Goodhart-Rendel, 'Every man might have his fancy – he need no longer be ashamed of taking simple pleasure in the ornate. The tawdry of the fairground was no sin; why should only gin-palaces exuberate?'[12]

Further pattern books published in the 1840s by T. King and Nathaniel Whittock mainly show shop fronts which existed at the time, with a wide variety of styles, including an Egyptian chemist's in Great Russell Street. The front of Fortnum and Mason in Piccadilly was described with fine insouciance as being in 'the Palladian or Italian style of architecture', although we should call it neo-Jacobean. It was built in 1834–35 by an unknown architect, and survived until 1926 when the present shop by Wimperis and Simpson replaced it. A comparable exercise in seventeenth-century style was Swan and Edgar's front in Piccadilly Circus, designed by Frederick Hering, which also survived until the 1920s.

Nathaniel Whittock subscribed to the picturesque doctrine of stylistic association, believing that the pure classic should be reserved for buildings or shops connected with learning and the arts. He upbraided contemporary designers for their lack of imagination, suggesting that 'some of the first-rate drapers who deal extensively in Indian goods, would be most properly distinguished by a splendid Indian front, selected from some of the gorgeous temples and pagodas that grace the banks of the Ganges.'[13] He thought Gothic (p. 66) was appropriate for goldsmiths, watch and clockmakers, printsellers, surgeons, chemists and druggists, and encouraged all shopmen to have their fronts richly painted, noting that the reticent style of the recent past (1835) was for all shops to be painted in imitation of white veined marble.

Among other constituents of the 'fancy style' was Louis XIV, popularised by Benjamin Dean Wyatt in the decoration of Crockford's. It was a favourite style of the upholsterers who practised as the chief agents of interior decoration – firms such as

Saunders and Woolley of Regent Street (p. 67), whose shop front
Whittock praised for 'a very splendid effect without being gaudy,
and quite appropriate for so showy a business'. It continued the
Regency taste for imitation materials, with ironwork painted to
imitate bronze, and gilt carving. Whittock recommended the style as
being cheaper than it looked, since 'compo' and papier mâché were
used instead of real carving.

Palm-tree columns like those on Saunders and Woolley's front
seem to have been a short-lived fashion, but some existed until the
1960s in a two-storey cast-iron shop front in Norwich (p. 68), a
miniature Crystal Palace dating probably from the 1850s.

Whittock also noted that 'The great improvement that has taken
place in the manufacture of plate glass, enables the glazier to
introduce squares of any dimensions at moderate price.' This was to
have long-term consequences on shop-front design, but as Mary
Eldridge writes, 'The introduction of plate glass was not, it seems,
accompanied by any violent break with traditional shop-front
design.' The drapers and outfitters in Regent Street and Oxford
Street hastened to enlarge their windows, so that by 1864 an article
in *Chambers' Journal* could write that 'Enormous plate-glass
windows, gilded or polished brass frames, expensive mirrors,
polished mahogany frames and all sorts of fancy woodwork,
sometimes crystal columns ... these are the necessary decorations of
a fashionable London shop of the middle of the nineteenth
century.'[14]

It was just such designs that A. W. N. Pugin caricatured in *The
True Principles of Pointed Architecture* in 1841, describing how
'Every linen-draper's shop apes to be something after the palace of
the Caesars; the mock stone columns are fixed over a front of plate
glass to exhibit the astonishing bargains; while low-ticketed goods
are hung out over the trophies of war.' Pugin's suggestion for a
grocer's shop, published in *An Apology for the Revival of Christian
Architecture* in 1843, has two Gothic windows pierced in a stone

façade. Such sobriety would not have succeeded in Regent Street in the 1840s.

Plate Glass and Glitter

The new plate-glass fronts introduced a different scale to the shop front. The stallboard at the base of the window virtually disappeared, and the shop front was carried much higher up, as can be seen in Tallis's 1847 view of Harvey's in Ludgate Hill (p. 68), next door to Papworth's chinoiserie. The central door is set back deeply in the façade, with display windows curving inwards, the prototype of the 'arcade' effect favoured by drapers as a means of drawing in customers. The bent plate glass in this front was 'the wonder of all London when it was first put up'.[15] Mahogany replaced pine for the mullions, allowing thinner glazing bars, to be succeeded in turn by brass.

A French method for covering a wooden core with a veneer of sheet brass was introduced in England in 1838 or 1839, according to the article in *Chambers' Journal*. The wood was strengthened with an iron tongue, providing a rebate for fixing the glass, while the brass could be kept in a high state of polish, although gilded and bronzed cast-iron remained common, and was cheaper. The latter material is used in one of the few surviving shops of this mid-century type, Asprey's in Old Bond Street (p. 70), the earliest parts of which date from 1865. The glass panes, set in an arcaded frame, are of a size not produced before 1860. The lettered brass stall-plates are right down on pavement level. The result is highly impressive, although the upper part of the window cannot be used for display, merely lighting a mezzanine inside the shop. A favoured effect with cast-iron columns was to form them as a barley-sugar twist, an example of which can be seen in Great Queen Street, Covent Garden.

Cast iron was used throughout the second half of the nineteenth century to provide ornamental cresting for shop fronts, either in

Gothic or classical style, a good example of the latter being a
rainceau scrolled cresting over Attenborough's the silversmiths and
jewellers in High Holborn. At Witney in Oxfordshire there are two
cast-iron shop fronts with exuberant ornament, both obviously
supplied by the same manufacturer (p. 69). These are dated by *The
Buildings of England* to c.1870, but their vocabulary of ornament is
more typical of the 1850s.

Among designers not afraid to plunge into the commercial world
was Owen Jones, famous for his studies of the Alhambra Palace and
of Egyptian ornament. His design for Chappell's, New Bond Street,
was described as 'purest Alhambra – even to the letters on the
stallboard'.[16] The same style was used for Sangster's in Cheapside,
and there is a drawing by Jones for Nos. 36–38 Oxford Street
(Jackson and Graham) (p. 72) with highly coloured ornament.
Henry-Russell Hitchcock points out the similarity of certain shop
front designs of this period with the decoration of stamped and
embossed book jackets, in 'the curious flowing plasticity of the
ornament, interrupted occasionally by sharply linear elements'.[17]

For humbler shop fronts, the flattened arched top had by this
time become a common feature, with three or four panes of glass
running to the full height of the window, held by mullions of a fin-
like profile. A good run of these shops can be seen in Museum
Street, London (p. 71), probably dating from the 1850s when the
houses of earlier date were given stucco fronts to modernise them.
The tall panes probably corresponded to the size of the shutters
fitted at night.

Architect versus Shopfitter

It is difficult to trace the evolution of shop front design past the
introduction of plate glass into the third quarter of the nineteenth
century, as so few examples of everyday shopfronts survive. A
magnificent exception is James Smith and Sons' umbrella shop at
No. 53 New Oxford Street, a unique survival of the gaudy,

attention-grabbing shop fronts of the 1870s, with every space crammed with coloured lettering painted on the back of glass, and lettering on the brass fascia plates (p. 74). Oxford Street and the Strand were filled with shops of this character until 1914. The reaction from the architectural profession to this style of shopfitter's work was to urge the use of solider materials, which did not attempt to deceive the eye. The Gothic Revival encouraged the use of solid timber, with stop-chamfer ornaments. An attempt to get away from the attenuated classical design typical of all shopfitters' work of this time is seen in *Street Architecture* by Victor Delassaux and John Elliott (1855) which has designs of French Second Empire style, as well as emulating the carpenters of the middle ages, praiseworthy because 'not a single stuck-on ornament is to be found in their work, in which only decorated utility can be discovered.'

Thornton's Bookshop at No. 11 Broad Street, Oxford, is a modest example of the style. Something more extravagant of a reforming Gothic kind can be seen at No. 6 Bow Lane, in the City of London (p. 73). In 1870, *Building News* commended some new shop fronts in Villiers Street, London, with flattened brick arches carried on solid brick piers, but felt that they were unlikely to have general appeal, since 'the shopkeeper requires his gaping chasm and his plate glass.'[18] A compromise favoured in architectural circles was to set the plate glass back behind the line of the columns, giving rather less the appearance which for decades had vexed architects, of solid masonry carried above a void of plate glass.

By the 1880s, with the popularisation of the 'Queen Anne' style, the tide was turning against the reign of plate glass, in favour of greater diversity and intricacy of ornament. An example was set on the Grosvenor Estate in Mayfair with the shop of Thomas Goode, china seller, at No. 35 South Audley Street. Begun in 1875, this shop front was designed as an integral part of the terracotta house fronts by Ernest George and Harold Peto, with solid-looking pilasters, even though the plate-glass windows are hardly broken up with

glazing bars. The automatic doors, which still survive, were a
remarkable novelty.

The style was adopted at the insistence of the Duke of
Westminster. George and Peto went on to build the shops in Mount
Street, with apartments above, such as those at Nos. 104–119 (p. 75),
dating from 1886. These have flattened arches in terracotta, and a
simple glazing pattern. This simplicity was lost as 'Queen Anne'
went down-market. In 1898 *Building News* noted that 'There is a
decided attempt to retrieve the vulgar obtrusiveness of plate glass by
making the framework more ornamental, by dividing the glass into
smaller panes, by shaping them ornamentally. A further attempt is
to recess the window or to make it bay-like, so as to introduce
outside recesses or lobbies.'[19] Examples of this style have not
survived well, although the left-hand half of a window in
Westbourne Grove – currently a Sue Ryder shop – which zig zags
like the folds of a screen, with a deeply set-back door, illustrates the
tendency admirably. The intricate use of curved glass and individual
display cases and windows can be seen in a pair of shops in
Moorgate in the City of London, of *c.*1900 (p. 79). One of the best
examples of the style is Kirkland's Bakery, now a café, in Hardman
Street, Liverpool (p. 76).

Dating from 1903, but in a much older tradition of freely adapted
'Louis' style, is the elaborate mahogany and brass shop front of the
Savoy Taylors Guild in the Strand (p. 81).

Drapers and Grocers

The luring of the customer from one item in the window display to
another, and so by stages in through the shop door, was a speciality
of drapers' shops, with their various departments. Fred W. Burgess,
author of *The Practical Retail Draper* (1912), mistrusted architects
who were 'apt to think more of the architectural beauty of the
building they plan than of its real usefulness for trade purposes'.
Burgess favoured a deep arcade, possibly containing a completely

glazed circular island window for 'model gowns', with the firm's name in mosaic tiling underfoot. The elaboration of window displays was immense, including historical tableaux and 'artistic effects' built up with white and embroidered handkerchiefs. An account of work in a shop of this kind in Folkestone, drawn from the author's personal experience, is found in *Kipps* by H. G. Wells.

Burgess proclaimed the superiority of polished gun-metal sash frames and mahogany woodwork, and advocated the use of sunblinds so that 'shoppers can pause for a few moments, and, out of the heat of the sun's rays, enjoy examining the contents of the windows so delightfully shaded.' The space on the pavement was also put to use for the display of 'garden furniture, tents, awnings, trunks, travelling requisites and a great many other goods'. In East Dulwich Road there are cast iron poles set in front of a row of shops, presumably to carry awnings shading this additional display space.

Although there must be a number of good arcade shops surviving in different parts of the country, many have vanished. Remembering Edwardian Tottenham, H. G. Hawkes wrote that 'The old in-and-out serpentine walks of extended shop fronts have gone. Mainly drapery establishments, they crammed a multitude of items of feminine apparel with large price cards all ending in the bait of $11^3/_4d$. to convince the buyer of economy.'[20] Examples of a later period are Bluston's in Kentish Town High Street and O. and C. Butcher in Aldeburgh High Street, both of which appear to be refits of earlier arcades.

The particularisation of the window display also applied for grocers, who, like drapers, considered themselves a higher class of independent retailers. By 1900 they were under pressure from Co-Operative stores in the north of England and multiple stores like Sainsbury's and David Greig in the London area, and had to work to retain their 'carriage trade'. It was equally a matter of social status among the customers as to which shops they patronised. New shop fronts were thought to appeal to lady customers, combined with a refit of the interior. Writing in *The Modern Grocer*, a five-volume compendium of 1919, Edward Maund considered that

> the old-fashioned shop front with its small panes of glass, the heavy woodwork, the floor approached from the entrance by steps, the ugly fittings with candle lockers, the square cannisters, the old tea-pot shaped treacle cisterns, the tee-shaped iron hangers for hand scales, titler shelves, sugar choppers and blocks, the high standard scales, (often screwed down with a nut to the counter), sugar mills and old signs, like the dip-candles which were found among them, are things of the past.

Maund illustrates the shopman's dream front (p. 84) – thirty-two feet long (the result of throwing two shops into one), with five distinct windows for grocery (left), provisions (right), wines and spirits in the centre, and 'bent plate-glass returns for confectionery, green fruit, toilet requisites, hardware etc'. The light sliding sashes of the provision window enabled the window to be redressed each morning with a display of 'poultry, sausages, rashers, cooked food etc'. To attract the pedestrian, the window display would benefit from the use of 'art-coloured majolica pedestals, flower-pots, figures, and other pottery, combined with ferns, palms, etc.'

Stylistically, Maund's shop front suggests the taste of 1900 rather than 1919, with its repoussé copper stall-plates, gold letters and 'artistic Louis pediment over the centre of the fascia'. For smaller shop fronts, he noted that the maximum display value should be got from the window by 'showing as much glass as possible and as little wood', the very thing to which architects had ineffectually objected for fifty years or more. By creating an ornamentally glazed 'clerestory' above the large plate-glass panes, shopfitters attempted to get the best of both worlds, using thin hardwood details. This was the style of Montague Burton, 'The Tailor of Taste', seen in the Bath shop photographed in the 1950s (p. 85). The design of this woodwork easily slid from 'Louis' to art nouveau, with interlacing tendrils, seen in Fitzbillies, the bakers in Trumpington Street,

Cambridge, and in a more elaborate form in a shop in Market Street, Cambridge, with inserts of opalescent glass.

Other shop types demanding special architectural treatment were those specialising in perishable provisions such as fish, meat and milk. A hygienic look was desirable as concern grew about public health, and glazed terracotta or faience were used, giving scope for delightful tiled decorations supplied by the manufacturer. A fishmonger at No. 9 Howard Street, Glasgow has good mosaic panels of fish in the fascia, probably Edwardian. There is a fine survival of a butcher's in Cirencester, probably of the 1920s, and a butcher's with a white, brown and cream ceramic façade and internal painted panels of 1928 has recently been listed in Middlewich, Cheshire (p. 86). In London, a number of small dairies of the 1920s survive, like Evans's in Conway Street (p. 86) and Lloyd's in Amwell Street, the latter being a timber corner-shop with fine lettering. A much grander dairy, now a toyshop, is Davies's in New Cavendish Street (p. 87), fitted into an apartment building of 1902 with a broad stone arch. Because of their association with dairy farming, these shops were, as the names indicate, traditionally run by Welsh families.

Multiple Stores

The arrival around 1900 of multiple stores introduced a new era in retailing, and consequently in the design of shops. Whereas it had previously been rare for a shop to have more than one or two branches, the idea of standard products and prices affected grocery, clothes, shoes, chemists, stationers and other businesses, with names which still dominate high streets today: Sainsbury's, Marks and Spencer, Freeman Hardy and Willis, Boots and W. H. Smith expanded in newly developing suburbs and existing shopping streets. It was important that their shops should be readily identifiable, and welcome customers at 'both ends of the market'.

Sainsbury's, from small beginnings with market stalls, achieved a

standardised house-style for shop fronts and shop interiors around
1900. The joinery was of dark wood, with arched window-heads.
The company name appeared on the fascia board and again with
cut-out letters on a wrought iron balcony above (p. 88). The upper
part of Sainsbury's shops were nearly always hostels for the staff, so
this lettering did not interfere with the light of private tenants.
Standardisation extended to the style of the window display. Every
week a specimen window was dressed at the head office at
Blackfriars, and copied by all the branches. On Christmas Eve, the
whole shop would be dressed on the outside with geese and turkeys,
the common practice for all provision merchants. The last
Sainsbury's counter store of this kind, in Rye Lane, Peckham,
closed in 1982.

W. H. Smith's operated entirely from railway bookstalls until the
end of 1905, when an attempt by the Great Western Railway and
another railway company to raise their rents led to a boycott by
Smith's, who consequently had to build or take over shops in the
towns they already served. The strength of their newspaper rounds
gave them an established commercial position. The standard design
for shop fronts reflects the Edwardian reaction against the vulgarity
of plate glass, and shows the influence of the Arts and Crafts
movement in the small-paned clerestory windows with 'olde world'
bottle glass, the 'hand-wrought' look of the hanging lamps outside,
and the gilded Roman lettering designed by Eric Gill, and first
executed directly by him for the Paris branch of W. H. Smith's in
1903. The letter forms were debased over the years by insensitive
adaptation and finally abandoned, but nothing of equal quality has
taken their place.

The door was always central, with a deep splayed, funnel-like
entrance. The right hand side of this always had the 'bookstall' for
the quick sale of newspapers, and the intention was to attract
customers who would not normally think of entering a bookshop to
venture further inside. As the staff journal *Newsbasket* wrote in
1913 of the new shop in Wolverhampton,

The door of the shop is never in use, excepting on the very coldest of days; and, owing to the mildness of the weather this winter, has not yet been put on. This, together with the fact that the door jambs themselves can be removed, makes the doorway and the shop itself continuous. There is little doubt of the value of this idea of *suggestive* invitation; it needs only the addition of the *printed* invitation to induce even the shyest passer-by to enter.

The style of the entrance can be seen in the Kingsway branch in London, originally built in 1907. The crammed window dressing was typical for this period, and was hardly modified in the remodelling of this shop in 1938, although the change in style was in other respects drastic. Some W. H. Smith's shops in the 1920s were decorated with picture panels of coloured tiles in the poster style of Fred Taylor, and the enamelled sign of the Newsboy was invented in the house advertising studio by Septimus Scott. A typical Smith's of the 1920s has been restored, as part of Architectural Heritage Year 1975, at Newtown, Powys (p. 91). By this time natural oak rather than painted timber was the prevailing style, with stall-risers of Cotswold stone, which often looked incongruous when introduced in areas other than the Cotswolds, but added to the homely English effect. Sometimes heads of Shakespeare and Ben Jonson were introduced to give extra literary associations, and the Birmingham shop had a frieze of 'children playing in sylvan surroundings'. Sadly, these decorative attempts to raise the tone of the business now seem like relics of a lost civilisation. The shop in Newtown trades with modern stock, but is considered by the company to be less profitable than a fully modernised branch would be in the same position.

Smith's probably maintained the highest standard of design of any of the multiple shops before the war, although this cannot be said of the present. By 1930 there was a movement of opposition to the uniformity being imposed on small towns and villages. Patrick

Abercrombie, the town planner, wrote that 'Their brutal stock fronts botched on to older buildings, cutting half-way through the first-floor windows, bring a shout of town vulgarity that drowns the quiet charm of the place.'[21] A. Edward Hammond, an apologist for the multiple traders, thought such scruples exaggerated, although he admitted that the shopfitters often paid more attention to the demand of shopkeepers for more display space than to the conflicting needs of architectural propriety. Worse damage was done to historic towns when the older buildings were demolished entirely to make way for new shops. Woolworth's, Marks and Spencer and Burton's were particularly enthusiastic builders in the 1930s. High streets throughout Britain have taken a battering from the insensitivity of both large and small businesses during the twentieth century, and planning legislation is still weak in this respect. In the 1950s the Civic Trust made deliberate attempts to restore the small scale and diversity of the traditional English shopping street, notably in Magdalen Street, Norwich, for which the architectural co-ordinator in 1959 was Misha Black. This provided a model for similar schemes in Windsor, Burslem and Croydon.

Quality Street Revisited

W. H. Smith's shops were symptomatic of a nostalgic attitude to commercial design in Edwardian England. Architects began to renew their interest in shop fronts, seeing them as part of the comfortable Georgian style concurrently being revived in domestic design, and as such a necessary counterbalance to the artless vulgarity of the shopfitter.

Since large expanses of plate glass now indicated low quality goods, the obvious response for high quality traders was to revive the many-paned window and give their shops an air of long-established reliability and exclusivity. This was encouraged by the example of a few shops, like Lock's in St James's Street, which had never changed their simple late-Georgian fronts (p. 94). The shop front of Hatchards Bookshop in Piccadilly, for example, is a 1912 rebuilding of its predecessor (p. 95). The first photographic book of shop front designs, by Horace Dan and E. C. Morgan Wilmott, was published in 1907, praising Georgian examples and publishing new work, sometimes closely copied from Georgian prototypes. Even the superficially art-nouveau details, particularly in the clerestory stained glass, were absorbed into a prevailing neo-Georgian trend, although an unusual degree of independence is found in the Kodak shop at No. 40 West Strand by George Walton, commended for its clever use of lighting.

Classical elements were used in ways which hardly resembled eighteenth-century prototypes, like the single supporting column in the chemist's shop front at No. 11 Southampton Row, illustrated by Dan and Wilmot and still surviving, notable also for its unvarnished and unpainted woodwork. Among larger stores, Heals in Tottenham Court Road, designed by Smith and Brewer in 1916, was consistently praised for the restraint of its shop front, set back some six feet behind a colonnade (p. 100). This was replaced in 1938 by curved non-reflecting windows, and although these have been removed, the Department of Environment insisted in 1985 on the retention of the original 'arcade'.

Art Deco and Modernism

The neo-Georgian tendency continued strongly into the 1920s, as seen in *Shop Fronts* by Frederick Chatterton, published in 1927, but the attraction of modern French designs in the art deco style of 1925, by designers such as Suë et Mare, was beginning to be felt in England. In 1907, Dan and Wilmott thought of the metal shop front as existing hitherto 'only as an outstanding protest against its own existence', but bronze became a favourite material for high-quality fronts, possibly in imitation of American examples. Kingsway was fitted with bronze shop fronts before 1914, and they were often used by the Post Office, for example in Albemarle Street, in the

1920s. Achille Serre, a chain of dyeing and cleaning shops, favoured bronze for ease of maintenance. One of the best survivors of a decorated luxury shop of the 1920s is Ciro at No. 95 Buchanan Street, Glasgow (p. 102).

Joseph Emberton (1889–1956), an architect whose father kept a draper's shop, introduced the angular Parisian 'Jazz modern' to London in 1926 with the shop front of Madelon Chaumet in Berkeley Square (p. 103), and soon developed a chain of shops in similar style for Lotus and Delta Shoes. Shop fronts were an important means for introducing the modern movement in architecture to Britain. In Vienna in the early 1900s Adolf Loos had used shop and café design as a means of taking modern design into the streets. *The Architecture of Shops* by A. Trystan Edwards (1933) finishes with examples by Raymond McGrath of shop fronts which aim to provide nothing more than a neutral setting for window display, but these had been preceded by the Helena Rubinstein Salon in Grafton Street, Mayfair (p. 104), designed in 1928 by Ernö Goldfinger, a Hungarian practising in Paris who was to settle in England in 1934 and design several more distinguished shop fronts. The shop fronts by Wells Coates for Cresta Silks were frequently illustrated, particularly when illuminated by night. Careful attention was given to the use of neon lighting, using thin coloured tubes, an effect which can still be seen on Simpsons in Piccadilly. Among the few survivors of this group of smaller early modernist shops is No. 115 Cannon Street, by Walter Gropius and Maxwell Fry (1936), recently restored (p. 107).

Modernism was far from sweeping the field in the 1930s. Raymond Erith and Sir Albert Richardson designed some fine late-Georgian style shops in fashionable London streets; a charming example is Culpeper's the Herbalist in Bruton Street, designed by Basil Ionides in 1931. With a wide range of styles, architects made a more positive contribution to shop front design between the wars than at any time before or since. The nostalgia for old shops progressed from the eighteenth to the nineteenth century, as can be seen in the lithographs by Eric Ravilious for *High Street* (1939), showing a delightful variety of typical small shops (p. 110).

Shopfitters' Modern

The majority of shop front designs remained in the hands of shopfitting firms, who rapidly absorbed the changing styles of the inter-war period. Favoured materials were Vitrolite, a self-coloured glass, usually black, pale green or orange, and chrome metalwork and lettering. Stall risers were often of mottled Aberdeen Granite, highly polished. Other stone and marble veneers were also popular. The shop front was intended to shine by day and night, with the assistance of back-lit letters or internally illuminated fascias. Examples of this style survive, and are now sufficiently rare to be worth preserving, like the 'Modiste' in St Andrew's Street, Cambridge, with its sun-rise glazing, or the branches of Kennedy's sausage shops in Camberwell and Peckham.

The enterprising shopfitters Pollard's took out a licence for a French system of non-reflective glazing which became popular in the 1930s, using curved plate-glass in various combinations. With weak internal light, there was a continual problem in seeing deep into a show room from the opposite side of the street. Pollard's curved windows were used by Joseph Emberton at Simpson's in Piccadilly (1936), and by Edward Maufe in refitting the Heals colonnade in Tottenham Court Road in 1938. A complete Pollard's shop front with the windows, black vitrolite and chrome lettering is Fox's umbrella shop in London Wall (Plate 108). These windows were expensive, and inhibited the display of certain kinds of goods, although a new one was installed in the Wedgwood showroom in Wigmore Street in recent years to match an earlier example. It was reported that a non-reflecting window had to be removed in Manchester in the 1930s because mothers caused an obstruction by lifting their small children over the stallboard to touch the glass and prove that it was really there.

Post War

The tendency of shop front design in the 1950s was towards further simplification. The fashion for black vitrolite fascias with chrome relief lettering continued, but shops otherwise had a drab 'Utility' look. English shops ignored both the decorative style of the Festival of Britain and the stylish modern designs of Italy in these years. With the shop front reduced to a neutral frame, attention was concentrated, occasionally with wit and stylishness, on the interior. Writing in 1957, Herbert Taylor considered that 'the over-all picture of shop design whether in provincial, suburban or central London Streets is one of saddening mediocrity.'[22]

The same could be said of the 1960s, with a few exceptions, such as the remarkable shop front of the Grima Jewellers shop in the Cavendish Hotel, Jermyn Street (p. 111), designed by G. H. and G. P. Grima in 1966 and constructed from large pieces of rough-hewn slate fixed to a framework, with little display windows in the gaps. The 'Swinging London' era produced some amusing ephemera of shopfitting, notably the King's Road boutique 'Granny Takes a Trip' with the front half of a car apparently bursting through the window, but little that can be called architecture. The legacy of the Sixties which still afflicts us is the standard aluminium shop front with an internally illuminated plastic box sign, usually with lettering in a crude sanserif, placed without regard for scale or spacing. Shopfronts like these contribute to the sense of indeterminate squalor in so many British streets (p. 112–3).

The revival of shop front design, insofar as such a thing has taken place, must be credited to the conservation movement, and the willingness of designers to take their inspiration from the past. The timber 'Gothick' front by John Prizeman at No. 32 Long Acre (1975) – originally Bertram Rota's bookshop – was a pioneer, and Ian MacCaig, working for the GLC Historic Buildings Division, followed this success with bold neo-Georgian designs in James Street, Covent Garden (p. 114). One of the best modern classical designs is

Trotter's the Opticians in George Street, Edinburgh (p. 115), using subtle modification of the Ionic capital to suggest spectacles.

'Period' shop fronts, usually suggesting the late nineteenth century, have become the stock-in-trade of multiple stores cultivating the image of long-established reliability and good taste, much as 'Quality Street' shop fronts were favoured in the 1920s. Laura Ashley, Crabtree and Evelyn and Penhaligon's have helped to humanise shopping streets with painted timber detailing, even if it is not always carried out to a very high standard. In York, for example, the replacement of modern shop fronts in streets like High and Low Petergate and Stonegate, already rich in Georgian shop fronts, by present-day 'period' designs, certainly helps the street picture, but the lack of carved or moulded ornament in the new-comers immediately sets them apart. In such cases, the bolder the simple profiles the better, especially if reinforced by good colour and lettering. In a number of towns, notably Harrogate and Halifax, the conservation officers of local councils have started schemes for the improvement of shop fronts, restoring historical features to complete mutilated original examples, and stimulating better quality in new designs.

Meanwhile, high fashion seems to have abandoned the shop front entirely. The upper part of Sloane Street consists almost entirely of huge sheets of plate glass, and this look is emulated in the proliferating branches of Next all over the country. As in the 1930s, chain stores, however good their house style of design may be, are in danger of making all shopping streets across the country look the same. In Bath certain well-known chains have been compelled to adapt to the historic surroundings. Although an atmosphere of fake history is undesirable, shop fronts should not disregard the architecture above and around them. Diversity, colour and even vulgarity are part of the tradition of shop front design and should not be swamped by corporate good taste any more than by the shopfitter's lowest common denominator.

NMR = National Monuments Record: Royal Commission on
Historical Monuments

THE OLD BULK SHOP, TEMPLE BAR, LONDON. Probably early
seventeenth-century. One of the famous last survivors of a primitive
type of shop, demolished 1846. (*Museum of London*)

NO. 34 HAYMARKET, LONDON , c.1754. A notable survival of a
deep-bowed shopfront, before the Building Act of 1774. Fribourg
and Treyer occupied the shop from 1754 until the late 1970s. (*Paul
Barkshire*)

NO. 11 NORTON FOLGATE, LONDON. A bow-fronted design with the classical elements reduced in scale (demolished). (*Greater London Photograph Library*)

NO. 4 ST MARY'S STREET, STAMFORD, late eighteenth-century.
Flattened bows, with a concave curve over the door, closely
resembling designs by William and James Pain. (*NMR*)

NO. 15 CORNHILL, LONDON (now in Museum of London), *c.* 1770.
(Watercolour by Philip Norman, 1926. *Museum of London*)

facing page, top Double bow-fronted shop, formerly in CREEK STREET, GREENWICH, now in Museum of London, *c.* 1820. A late example of the form. (*Museum of London*)

facing page, bottom A simple but elegant bow front at NO. 2 ABBEY STREET, BATH, photographed in 1945. Note the fine area grating. (*NMR*)

above NO. 56 ARTILLERY LANE, LONDON, *c.* 1756–7. A spirited architectural composition with fine carving. (*NMR*)

BERRY BROS RUDD LTD., ST JAMES'S STREET. One of the few
shops still using wooden shutters. The two right-hand bays of this
front are genuine, the rest is a clever 1930s imitation. (*Paul
Barkshire*)

NO. 1 TERRACE WALK, BATH, *c.* 1750. A regular architectural composition using classical pattern books, altered after the time of this photograph. (*NMR*)

BOOT'S THE CHEMISTS, 58 LONDON ROAD, SOUTHWARK, 1904.
A demonstration of the publicity potential of roller shutters.
(*Museum of London*)

LXXI

Tradecard of John Flude, NO. 3 GRACECHURCH STREET, 1780s, showing jewellers and pawnbrokers shop. Tradecards and, later, packaging used images of shopfronts to identify the business. (*Museum of London*)

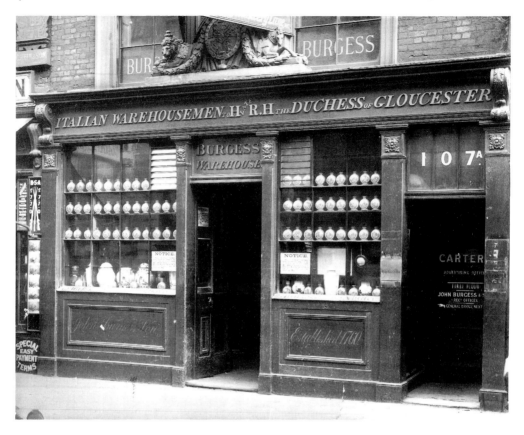

above NO. 107 STRAND, LONDON. Early nineteenth-century. A pilastered flat front with fine shadowed lettering and royal arms. Demolished. (*Greater London Photograph Library*)

facing page TWINING'S TEA WAREHOUSE, STRAND, early nineteenth-century. The Chinamen survive, but the royal arms have gone. (*Greater London Photograph Library*)

NO. 30 TRINITY STREET, CAMBRIDGE, late eighteenth-century. A handsome arched shopfront with 'Gothick' glazing. (*Courtesy of Heffer's Bookshop*)

NO. 37 STONEGATE, YORK, early nineteenth-century. The elaborate composition mouldings are typical of shopfronts in York. (*NMR*)

WOBURN WALK, LONDON, 1822. A parade of matching shops,
developed by Thomas Cubitt in Greek Revival style. (*Alan Powers*)

MARKET PLACE, CHEADLE, STAFFORDSHIRE. A rare example of identical shop fronts in a row, dated 1819. In need of preservation. (*Alan Powers*)

facing page, left ROYAL OPERA ARCADE, PALL MALL, LONDON, architect John Nash, 1816–18. Small luxury shops in a setting inspired by Parisian examples. (*Alan Powers*)

facing page, right MONTPELIER WALK, CHELTENHAM, architect William Knight, *c.* 1840. An elegant parade of shops, linked with an arcade and pump room. The Greek caryatids act as pilasters between the shops. (*Alan Powers*)

above BURLINGTON ARCADE, PICCADILLY, LONDON, architect Samuel Ware, 1819. London's most successful arcade still provides a convenient pedestrian route. (*Alan Powers*)

NO. 37 SOHO SQUARE, LONDON, *c.* 1820. A fine example of a
Greek Doric shopfront. (*Alan Powers*)

NO. 209 HIGH HOLBORN, LONDON, *c.* 1820. A slimmer Doric
order with a less correct entablature than the Soho Square example
(demolished). (*Greater London Photograph Library*)

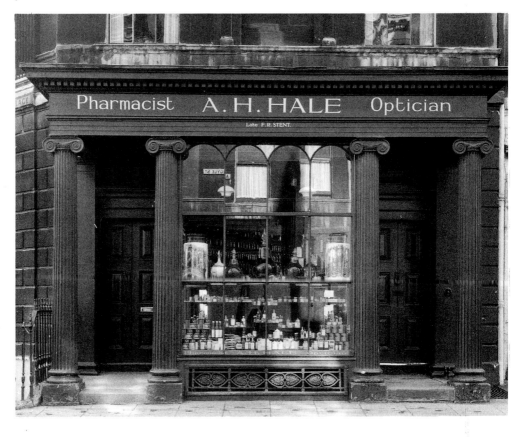

NO. 8 ARGYLE STREET, BATH, *c.* 1828. An Ionic portico glazed to
form the front part of a shop, with an early form of plate glass.
(*NMR*)

NO. 13 ST MARY'S STREET, STAMFORD, 1849. This shop is one of a matching pair, part of a grand civic composition never realised. (*NMR*)

facing page, top   FRANK COOPER, 84 HIGH STREET, OXFORD, *c.* 1840. A well-proportioned classical shop front with a fine interior. (*Alan Powers*)

facing page, bottom   NO. 43 EASTCHEAP, LONDON, *c.* 1840. A corner shop treated with two distinct elevations. (*Alan Powers*)

above   NO. 1 RICHMOND AVENUE, BARNSBURY, LONDON, *c.* 1835. The builder of this shop appears to have made a liberal selection from a catalogue of ornaments. (*Alan Powers*)

facing page NO. 8 LUDGATE HILL, LONDON, design by
J. B. Papworth, 1822. An example of picturesque associational
design for a tea merchant (demolished). (*British Architectural
Library*)

above WHITECHAPEL BELL FOUNDRY, NO. 34 WHITECHAPEL
ROAD, LONDON. An elegant front comparable to Papworth's
designs, probably *c.* 1820. (*Paul Barkshire*)

top NO. 43 FLEET STREET, LONDON, design by J. B. Papworth,
1827–8. Simple and elegant classical details, (demolished). (*British
Architectural Library*)

above NO. 115 PICCADILLY, LONDON, design by J. B. Papworth,
1824. A discreet, almost domestic, showroom for an upholsterer,
(demolished). (*British Architectural Library*)

Design for shops in LIME STREET, LIVERPOOL by H. Lonsdale
Elmes, 1843. The Venetian window form provides an architectural
logic. (*British Architectural Library*)

facing page NO. 94 HOLBORN HILL, LONDON, design for console bracket by J. B. Papworth, 1829–30. A simple version of a feature which was to predominate in later nineteenth-century shop design. (*British Architectural Library*)

above Scrolled console brackets with river god heads, ST GILES'S STREET, OXFORD. Consoles were usually used to divide one shop from another in a row. (*Alan Powers*)

facing page, top   Nathaniel Whittock *On the Construction and Decoration of the Shop Fronts of London*, 1840. Gothic used as a solution to the design of narrow eight-foot shop fronts, and stylistically suitable for jewellers. (*British Library*)

facing page, bottom   Nathaniel Whittock's illustration of a way of overcoming restrictive covenants prohibiting the insertion of a shop front. Here, the windows are left intact, but have display cases mounted on the shutters inside. It is uncertain how the interior of the shop was lit. (*British Library*)

above   SAUNDERS AND WOOLLEY, REGENT STREET, from Nathaniel Whittock. 'A very splendid effect without being gaudy, and quite appropriate for so showy a business.' (*British Library*)

left NO. 9 LUDGATE HILL, LONDON, *c.* 1840. The tall windows of
bent plate glass, cast iron colonettes and richly ornamented cornice
made effective commercial use of new materials and methods
(demolished). (Engraving from John Tallis *London Street Views*
1840.)

right DAVEY PLACE, NORWICH, *c.* 1850. Two-storey shop front
with cast iron columns, apparently designed for workshops above
and display windows below (demolished). (*NMR*)

HIGH STREET, WITNEY, OXFORDSHIRE, *c.* 1870. An elaborate cast-iron shop front. There is another in Witney of the same pattern. (*Alan Powers*)

ASPREY, NEW BOND STREET. A fine survival of mid-Victorian plate glass. No. 166, to the right, is the original front of *c.* 1865, with a narrower centre bay for the door. These columns are wreathed with spiral ribbons, while later ones in the adjoining parts of the front are plain fluted. The stallboard is reduced to the lowest level. (*Alan Powers*)

Shops in MUSEUM STREET, BLOOMSBURY. Tall panes of plate glass,
with arched wooden heads, typical of the 1850s. (*Alan Powers*)

NOS. 36–38 OXFORD STREET, LONDON, design by Owen Jones,
c. 1850. Large sheets of plate glass are used, with the shop name on
a brass stallboard plate, near ground level. The pierced cast iron
grille in the stallboard allows some light into the basement. The
design is brightly coloured (demolished). (*British Architectural
Library*)

NO. 6 BOW LANE, CITY OF LONDON. An example of reformed
Gothic, designed with cast iron to show structure.

NO. 53 NEW OXFORD STREET, LONDON, after 1865. The lettering, painted on the back of glass panels, dominates the shop front, and the interior continues the glassy effect. The iron cresting above the fascia was a common late nineteenth-century feature, designed to catch the eye amidst the accumulation of other intricate details. The stallboard lettering has recently been successfully restored. (*Alan Powers*)

NO. 117 MOUNT STREET, LONDON, architect George and Peto
1886. The shop front is solidly constructed of pink terracotta and
integrated with the building above. The privilege of hanging game
outside in the refined atmosphere of Mayfair was fiercely fought for
by the original firm, which continues the practice. (*Alan Power*)

KIRKLAND'S, HARDMAN STREET, LIVERPOOL, *c.* 1890. A shop
front in 'Queen Anne' taste, with carved wooden spandrels. (*Alan
Powers*)

CASTLE STREÉT, LIVERPOOL, *c.* 1900. The Art Nouveau influence
is found in the upper part of the window, with insets of purple
glass. (*Alan Powers*)

NO. 123 CHEAPSIDE, LONDON, *c.* 1900. An elegant solution to a corner entrance, with curved plate glass, a mirrored soffit and tall mirror panels in the display windows. (*Alan Powers*)

NO. 67 MOORGATE, LONDON, *c.* 1900. The deep entrance is used for additional display cases, and serves both the shop and the chambers over it. (*Alan Powers*)

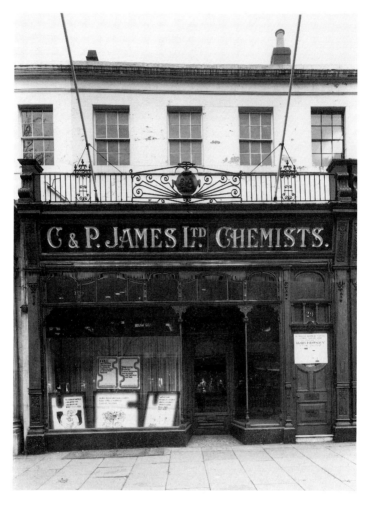

NO. 29, THE PROMENADE, CHELTENHAM. An example of shop-fitters' 'Queen Anne' with elaborate clerestory glazing. (*NMR*)

SAVOY TAYLORS' GUILD, STRAND, LONDON, 1903. The French
Rococo style enjoyed a continuous vogue for fashionable shops
from the 1840s onwards. (*Alan Powers*)

Shops in SICILIAN AVENUE, SOUTHAMPTON ROW, LONDON,
architect W. S. Wortley, 1905. These pretty projecting shop fronts
are well integrated into the architecture, and lend themselves to the
display of complete crocodile skins. (*Greater London Photograph
Library*)

Arcade at 213 KENTISH TOWN ROAD, LONDON, *c.* 1935. A late example of a plan-form typical of drapers' shops from the 1890s onwards. (*Alan Powers*)

Model shop front design from *The Modern Grocer*, 1919. The thin mahogany glazing details are typical of many shop fronts from the 1890s onwards. (*British Library*)

BURTON'S, STALL STREET, BATH, *c.* 1910. An early example of a chain store, with decorated clerestory glazing. (*NMR*)

facing page, top BUTCHER'S, MIDDLEWICH, CHESHIRE, 1928.
The splendid curved pediment is made from stock designs intended
for butchers. (*Alan Powers*)

facing page, bottom NO. 35 CONWAY STREET, LONDON, c. 1910.
Glazed terracotta was favoured for provision shops, and lent itself
to moulded and painted decoration. (*Alan Powers*)

bottom NOS. 14–16 NEW CAVENDISH STREET, LONDON, 1902.
Architect George Harvey. A dairy given a serious architectural
treatment with a strong arch which actually looks as if it could hold
up the building above. The Art Nouveau details may derive from
No. 37 Harley Street, designed by A. Beresford Pite.

SAINSBURY'S, 143 HIGH STREET, GUILDFORD, *c.* 1930. A typical
pre-war Sainsbury's shop, of a type introduced around 1900.
(*Courtesy of J. Sainsbury plc*)

SHOPPING PARADE, AMERSHAM, 1937. Sainsbury's promoted the development and took the central site, together with other national chains. The style of their shop front was by then very old-fashioned, but maintained for easy recognition. (*Courtesy of J. Sainsbury plc*)

ANFIELD PLAIN COOP., Beamish Museum, Co. Durham. A rebuilt
original Co-op typical of many northern shops. The iron and glass
pavement canopy is not original to this building. (*Courtesy Beamish
Museum*)

W. H. SMITH, NEWTOWN, MONTGOMERYSHIRE, 1927. This shop was restored to its original appearance in 1975, with oak structure, tile panels and Cotswold stone stall-riser. (*Courtesy of W. H. Smith Ltd.*)

A HIGH STANDARD OF APPEARANCE IN A SHOP PRODUCES HIGH-CLASS BUSINESS
WHICH IS BOTH PROFITABLE AND SATISFACTORY

above   W. H. SMITH, 11 KINGSWAY, LONDON, 1907. The early
Smith's shops were carefully designed and detailed on Arts and
Crafts principles. (*Courtesy of W. H. Smith Ltd.*)

facing page, top   The same shop remodelled in 1937. It has since
been further remodelled, and the deep arcade replaced by a
conventional shop window. (*Courtesy of W. H. Smith Ltd*)

facing page, bottom   The same shop today, showing a steady
decline in the quality of fascia lettering. (*Alan Powers*)

LOCK AND CO., ST JAMES'S STREET, *c*. 1810. By the early twentieth century, shop fronts like these were valued for their quaintness. (*Paul Barkshire*)

HATCHARD'S, PICCADILLY, 1912. This long-established business chose to perpetuate an old-fashioned Georgian image when rebuilding. (*Alan Powers*)

181 HIGH HOLBORN, *c.* 1820. Demolished before 1914 and acquired by the Museum of London. (*Greater London Photograph Library*)

OVERTON'S, ST JAMES'S. A close copy of No. 59, probably
installed in the 1950s. (*Alan Powers*)

KODAK LTD., NO. 40 WEST STRAND, *c.* 1899. Architect George Walton. Walton was a friend and collaborator of Charles Rennie Mackintosh. The Kodak shop shows the Arts and Crafts style tinged with Art Nouveau, and was admired for its clever use of natural and electric light. The style was meant to appear old-fashioned and quaint. (*British Architectural Library*)

MAPPIN AND WEBB, OXFORD STREET, 1908. Architects Belcher and
Joass. A fine commercial building, faced in Pentelic marble, on a
steel frame structure. The bronze shop front reflects French
fashions, but allows the columns to appear loadbearing (*NMR*)

HEALS, TOTTENHAM COURT ROAD, 1916. Architects Smith and
Brewer. The recessed shop window was much admired for its
discreet reticence. (*NMR*)

DARRACQ SHOWROOM, NEW BOND STREET, 1914. In the
Edwardian Beaux Arts style, the most modern at the time, and thus
suitable for luxury motor-cars. The shop front itself is underplayed,
but the building is composed as a whole to advertise the company
discreetly, compared to the extreme publicity given by the
contemporary Michelin building in the Fulham Road. (*NMR*)

NO. 95 BUCHANAN STREET, GLASGOW, *c.* 1925. A French-style
jewellers of bronze, with marble stallboard. Note the finely detailed
hanging sign. (*Alan Powers*)

MADELON CHAUMET, BERKELEY SQUARE, architect Joseph
Emberton 1926. An early example of the influence of the 1925 Paris
Exhibition of Decorative Arts, which was reflected in many shop
fronts. (*Architectural Association Slide Library*)

HELENA RUBENSTEIN SALON, GRAFTON STREET, LONDON, 1929.
Architect Erno Goldfinger. The first undecorated modern shop
front in London

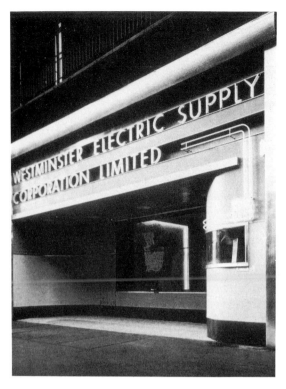

WESTMINSTER ELECTRIC SUPPLY CORPORATION LTD.
SHOWROOM, VICTORIA STREET, 1934 by E. Maxwell Fry. Modern
architecture to promote the modern power source. (*Architectural
Association Slide Library*)

GEORG JENSEN, NEW BOND STREET, 1930s. A reticent design
which lets the quality of the products speak for itself, with elegant
modern lettering and Danish crown. (*Architectural Association slide
Library, F. R. Yerbury photograph*)

NO. 115 CANNON STREET, 1936. Architects Walter Gropius and
E. Maxwell Fry. Originally Mortimer Gall electric goods
showroom, now sensitively restored with lettering echoing the
original. A bold asymmetrical design, using the favourite black
vitrolite of the period. (*Alan Powers*)

NO. 118 LONDON WALL, LONDON. A perfect example of 1930s shopfitting, with non-reflective window, and red-neon outline lettering against black vitrolite, with chrome details. (*Alan Powers*)

'LUCINDE', LOCATION UNKNOWN. Survivals of this style of
Hollywood moderne are increasingly rare. (*Architectural
Association Slide Library*)

Eric Ravilious, illustration to *High Street* by J. M. Richards, 1938.
This beautiful lithographed book recalled with affection the
Victorian shops surviving before the war. This is based on a real
shop in London selling diving equipment.

GRIMA JEWELLERS, JERMYN STREET, LONDON, architect A.
Grima, 1962. A remarkable attempt to break the conventions of
shop front design, using rough slate slabs bolted to a steel screen.

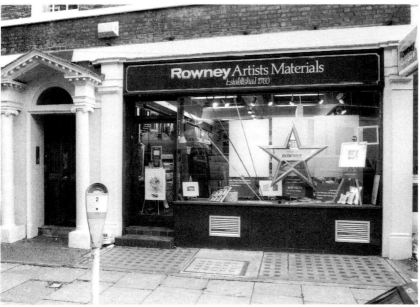

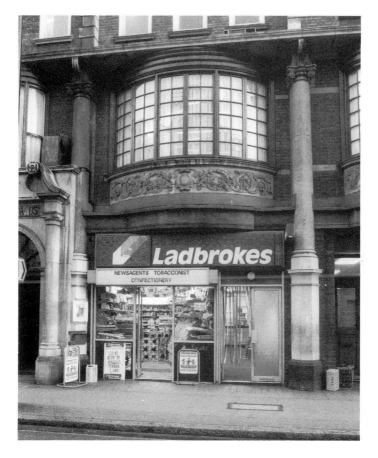

facing page, top UNDERWOOD'S, TOTTENHAM COURT ROAD, LONDON. A crude imposition of an unattractive house style

facing page, bottom ROWNEY'S, PERCY STREET, LONDON. Previously a plain modern front, it has, if anything, been made worse by a half-hearted attempt at 'heritage' lettering and colours. (*Alan Powers*)

above MORTIMER STREET, LONDON. Another house style completely at odds with a fine building

top THE POSTER SHOP, JAMES STREET, COVENT GARDEN.
Designed by Iain McCaig for the former GLC Historic Buildings
Division. One of the best neo-Georgian shop fronts of the 1980s.

above OPTICIANS, WIGMORE STREET, LONDON. A high-tech
modern design, perfectly suited to the modern block above, with a
sensitively lit and well-displayed window. (*Alan Powers*)

NO. 44 GEORGE STREET, EDINBURGH, architects Simpson and
Brown, 1987. This replaced a 1960s glass box front with a design
more suited to the classical street, incorporating lanterns from a still
earlier shop. The 'optician's order' of the ionic capitals is a typical
Post-Modernist joke, but not overdone. (*Alan Powers*)

REFERENCES

1. Dorothy Davis, *A History of Shopping*, p. 102.
2. *The Antiquary*, XIII, 1886, p. 35. Quoted in Davis *op. cit.* p. 103.
3. Daniel Defoe, *Tour Through the Whole Island of Great Britain*, 1724–27.
4. Neil McKendrick, *The Birth of a Consumer Society*, p. 32.
5. John Summerson, *Georgian London*, p. 128.
6. James Peller Malcolm, *Anecdotes of the Manners and Customs of London*, Volume 2, p. 402.
7. *ibid.*
8. S. von La Roche, *Sophie in London* (1786), ed. Clare Williams, p. 87.
9. McKendrick, *op. cit.* p. 21.
10. Henry Mayhew, *The Shops and Companies of London*, p. 100.
11. J. F. Geist, *Arcades*, p. 318.
12. H. S. Goodhart-Rendel, *English Architecture Since the Regency* (London, 1953) p. 70.
13. N. Whittock, *On the Construction and Decoration of the Shop Fronts of London* (1840).
14. Chambers' *Journal*, 8 October 1864, pp. 670–2.
15. Mayhew, *op. cit.*, p. 208.
16. *ibid.*
17. Henry-Russell Hitchcock, *Early Victorian Architecture in Britain*, p. 396.
18. 'Design in Shop Fronts' by W. H. R., *Building News*, 19 April 1870.
19. *Building News* LXXV, 1898, p. 811, quoted in Donald J. Olsen *The Growth of Victorian London* (London, 1976), p. 80.
20. H. G. Hawkes, *Tottenham Shops, a personal memory* (Edmonton Hundred Historical Society, 1983), p. 26.
21. *Commercial Art*, February 1930.
22. Herbert Taylor, 'Shops' in *Architectural Review*, CXXI, 1957, p. 104.

BIBLIOGRAPHY

Books

Adburgham, Alison, *Shops and Shopping 1800–1914* (London, 1964).

Bartram, Alan, *Fascia Lettering* (London, 1975).

Beeching, C. L. T. *ed.*, *The Modern Grocer and Provision Dealer* (London, 1919).

Burgess, P. W., *The Practical Retail Draper* (London, c. 1912).

Butler, R. E. and D. Hoy, *Over the Counter* (Edmonton Historical Society).

Chatterton, Frederick, *Shop Fronts* (London, 1927).

Civic Trust, *Some thoughts on the design of shopfronts presented in pictures* (London, 1963).

Dan, Horace and C. Morgan Wilmott, *English Shop Fronts Old and New* (London, 1907).

Davis, Dorothy, *A History of Shopping* (London, 1966).

Dean, David, *English Shopfronts from Contemporary Source Books 1792–1840* (reprints plates from I. & J. Taylor, *Designs for Shop Fronts*, 1792, J. Young, *A series of Designs for Shop Fronts*, 1828, J. Faulkner *Designs for Shop Fronts*, 1831, T. King, *Shop Fronts and Exterior Doors*, N. Whittock, *On the Construction and Decoration of the Shop Fronts of London*, 1840).

Delassaux, Victor and John Elliott, *Street Architecture* (London, 1855).

Edwards, A. Trystan, *The Architecture of Shops* (London, 1933).

Elliott, C. J. and Stanley, *The Modern Retailer* (London, 1937).

Evans, Bill and Andrew Lawson, *A Nation of Shopkeepers* (London, 1981).

Geist, Johann Friedrich, *Arcades, The History of a Building Type* (London, 1983).

Hammond, A. Edward, *Multiple Shop Organisation* (London, 1930).

Hitchcock, Henry-Russell, *Early Victorian Architecture in Britain* (London, 1954).

Jackson, Peter, *John Tallis's London Street Views 1838–1840* (London, 1969).

George Scharf's London (London, 1987).

Jeffreys, James B., *Retail Trading in Britain 1850–1950*.

McKendrick, Neil, John Brewer and J. H. Plumb, *The Birth of a Consumer Society* (London, 1982).

McGrath, Raymond and A. C. Frost,
Glass in Architecture and Decoration
(London, 1937).

Mayhew, Henry, *The Shops and
Companies of London* (London,
1865).

Ogden, William Sharp, *Mercantile
Architecture* (London, 1877).

RIBA Drawings Collection Catalogue,
George MacHardy: *The Office of J.
B. Papworth* (London, 1977).

Richards, J. M. and Eric Ravilious,
High Street (London, 1939).

Robinson, John Martin, 'Shop-Fronts'
in Alan Powers *ed., Real
Architecture* (London, 1987).

Summerson, John, *Georgian London*
(London, 1945).

Somake, Ellis E. and Rolf Hellberg,
Shops and Stores Today (London,
1956).

Survey of London passim.

Turner, Michael L. and David Vaisey,
Oxford Shops and Shopping (Oxford,
1972).

Westwood, Bryan and Norman, *Smaller
Retail Shops* (London, 1937).

Whittaker, Neville, *Shopfront* (Civic
Trust for the North-East), 1980.

Winstanley, Michael J., *The
Shopkeeper's World 1830–1914*
(London, 1983).

Articles

Eldridge, Mary, 'The Plate-Glass Shop
Front', *Architectural Review* CXXIII,
1958, pp. 192–5.

Tayler, Herbert, 'Shops', *Architectural
Review* CXXI, 1957, pp. 98–111.

Grundy, Joan, 'Inter-War Shop Fronts',
Thirties Society Journal No. 2, 1982,
pp. 41–4.

'The London Shop-Fronts', *Chambers'
Journal*, 8 October 1864, pp. 670–2.

Wheatley, Harry B. 'Old London Shop
Fronts', *Country Life* XXIV, 1908,
pp. 653–6.